COUNTRY SONGS
with a Classical Flair

16 SELECTIONS ARRANGED BY PHILLIP KEVEREN

— PIANO LEVEL —
INTERMEDIATE

ISBN 978-1-5400-9779-8

HAL•LEONARD®

Visit Hal Leonard Online at
www.halleonard.com

Visit Phillip at
www.phillipkeveren.com

Contact us:
Hal Leonard
7777 West Bluemound Road
Milwaukee, WI 53213
Email: info@halleonard.com

In Europe, contact:
Hal Leonard Europe Limited
42 Wigmore Street
Marylebone, London, W1U 2RN
Email: info@halleonardeurope.com

In Australia, contact:
Hal Leonard Australia Pty. Ltd.
4 Lentara Court
Cheltenham, Victoria, 3192 Australia
Email: info@halleonard.com.au

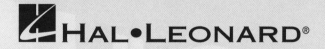

PREFACE

Using classical compositional devices, these iconic country songs have been developed into character pieces for piano solo. The term "classical" gets tossed about widely in the world of music. In this application, my guiding goal is to fashion an *arrangement* that feels more like a *composition* created expressly for the piano.

I hope these settings will enrich your enjoyment of music in general, and the pleasure of pursuing keyboard artistry in particular.

Sincerely,

Phillip Keveren

BIOGRAPHY

Phillip Keveren, a multi-talented keyboard artist and composer, has composed original works in a variety of genres from piano solo to symphonic orchestra. He gives frequent concerts and workshops for teachers and their students in the United States, Canada, Europe, Australia, and Asia. Mr. Keveren holds a B.M. in composition from California State University Northridge and a M.M. in composition from the University of Southern California.

CONTENTS

ALWAYS ON MY MIND

Words and Music by WAYNE THOMPSON,
MARK JAMES and JOHNNY CHRISTOPHER
Arranged by Phillip Keveren

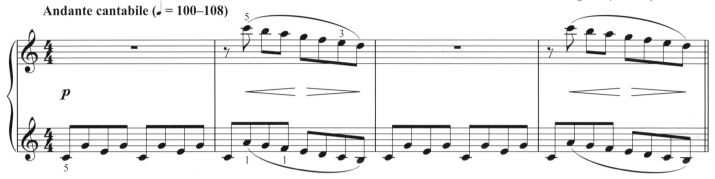

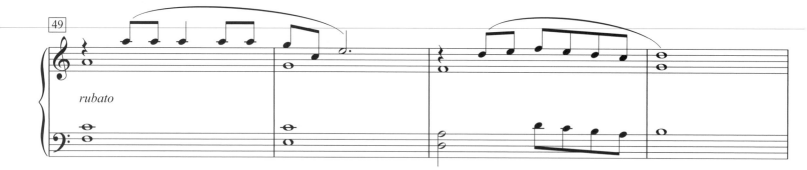

BY THE TIME I GET TO PHOENIX

Words and Music by
JIMMY WEBB
Arranged by Phillip Keveren

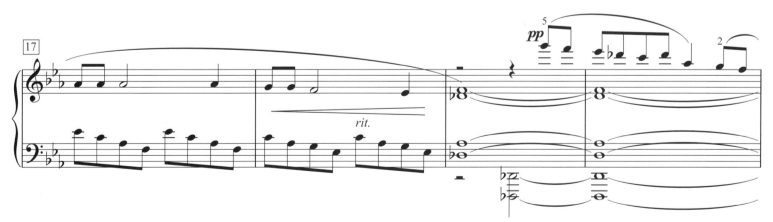

With more motion (♩ = c. 108)

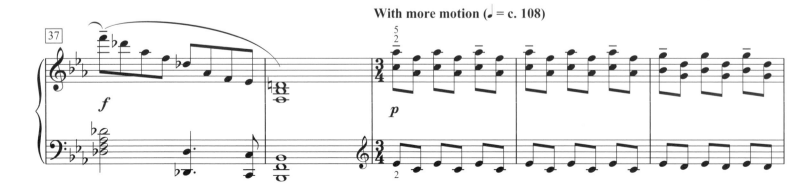

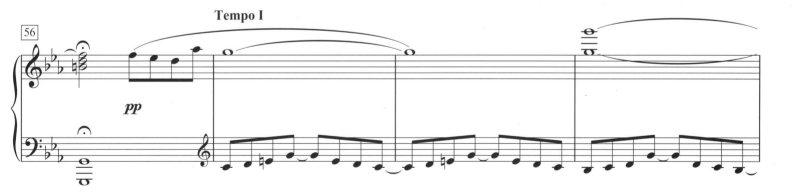

CRAZY

Words and Music by
WILLIE NELSON
Arranged by Phillip Keveren

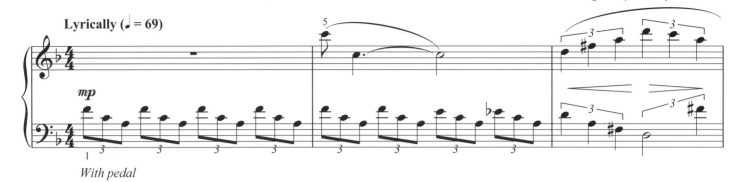

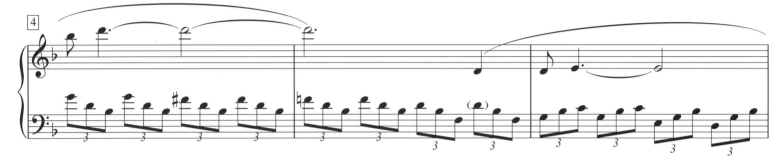

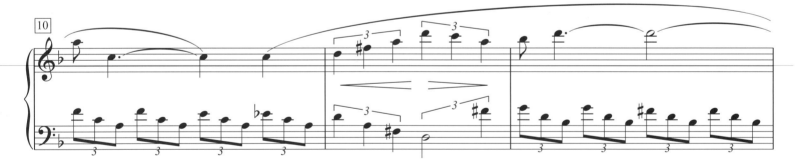

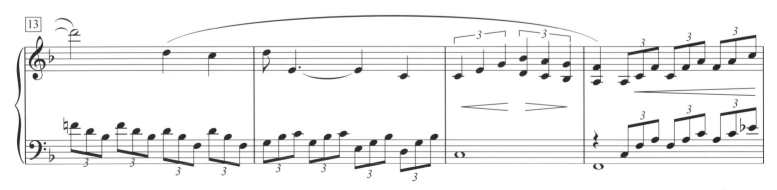

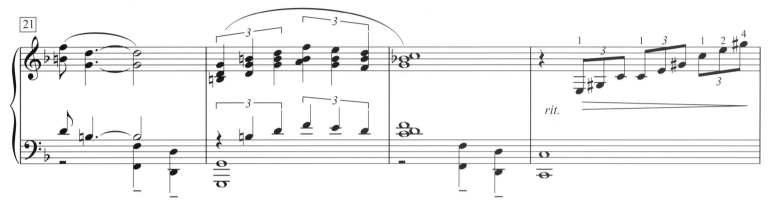

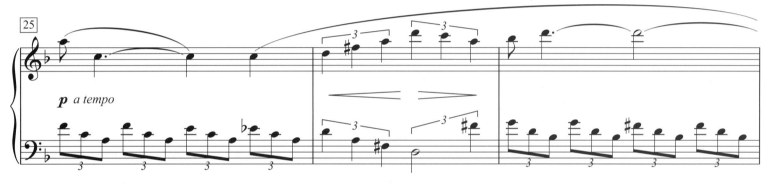

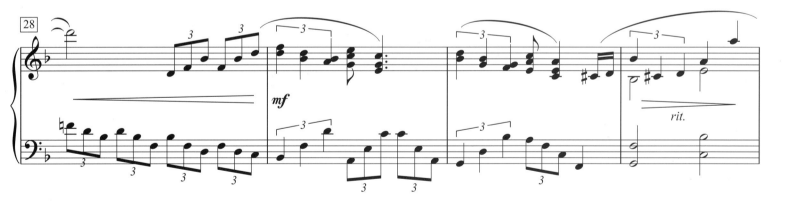

FOR THE GOOD TIMES

Words and Music by
KRIS KRISTOFFERSON
Arranged by Phillip Keveren

Bittersweet (♩ = c. 92)

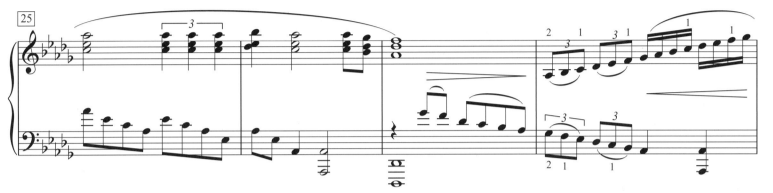

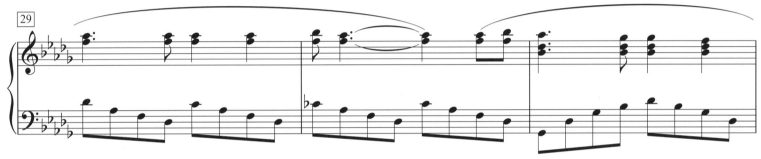

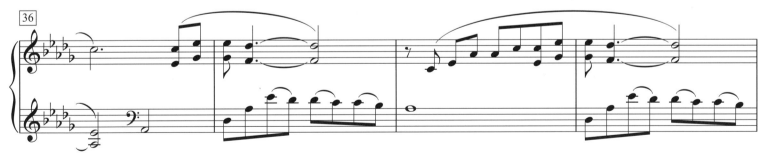

DON'T IT MAKE MY BROWN EYES BLUE

Words and Music by
RICHARD LEIGH
Arranged by Phillip Keveren

Gently flowing (♩. = 69)

FRIENDS IN LOW PLACES

Words and Music by DeWAYNE BLACKWELL
and EARL BUD LEE
Arranged by Phillip Keveren

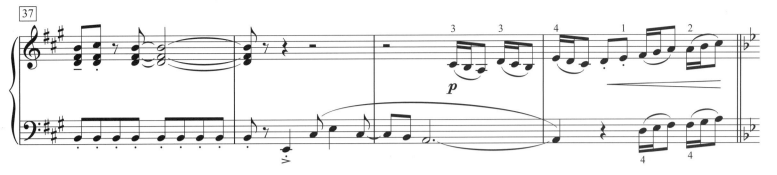

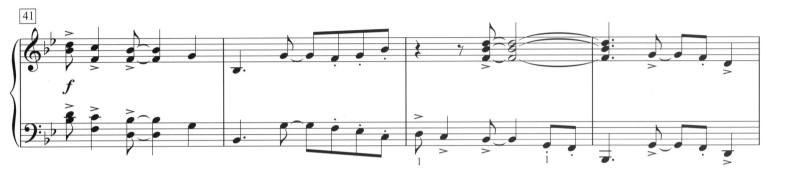

I HOPE YOU DANCE

Words and Music by TIA SILLERS
and MARK D. SANDERS
Arranged by Phillip Keveren

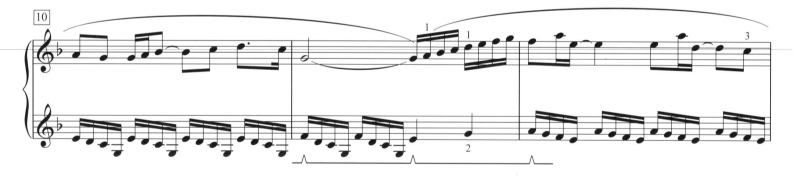

I WALK THE LINE

Words and Music by
JOHN R. CASH
Arranged by Phillip Keveren

Solemnly, with rubato ($\half = $ c. 60)

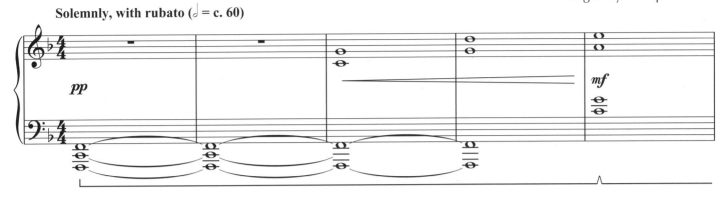

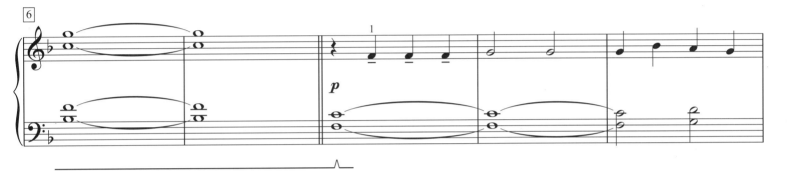

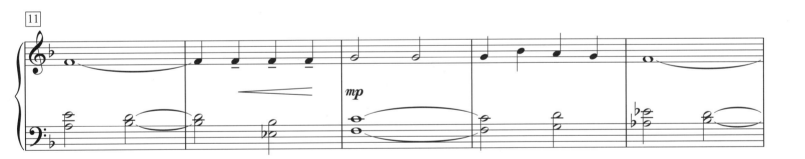

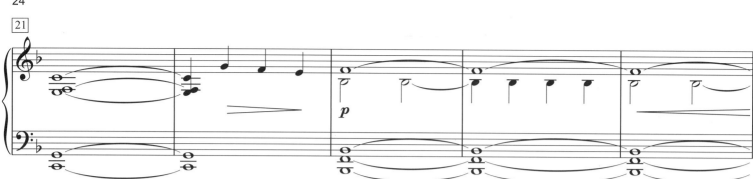

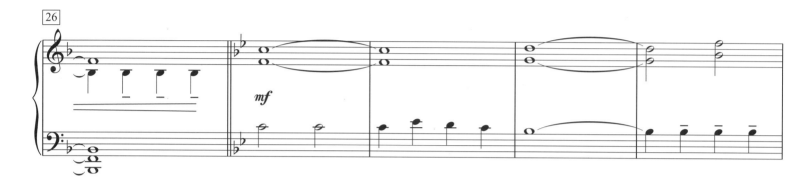

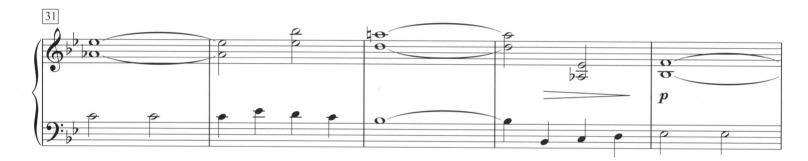

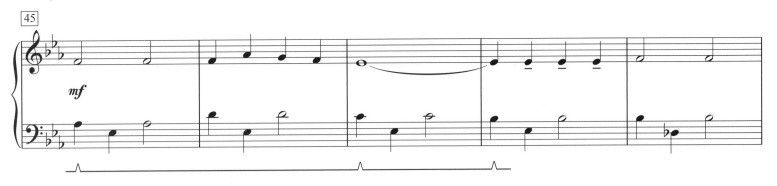

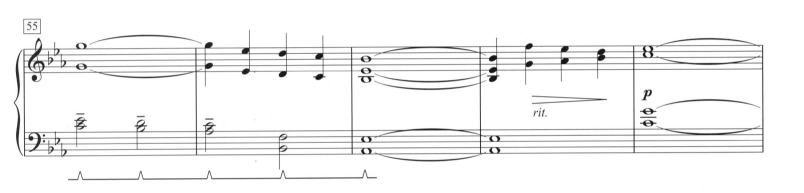

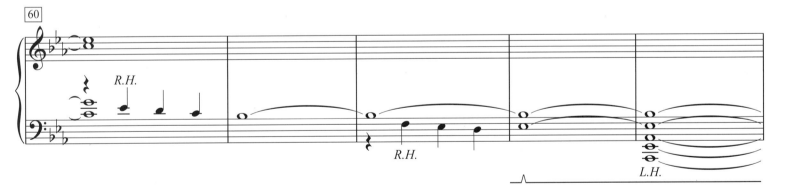

KING OF THE ROAD

Words and Music by
ROGER MILLER
Arranged by Phillip Keveren

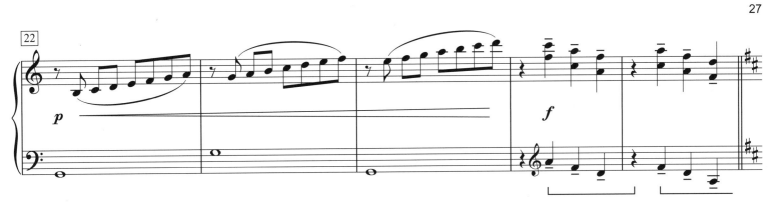

(I Never Promised You A)
ROSE GARDEN

Words and Music by
JOE SOUTH
Arranged by Phillip Keveren

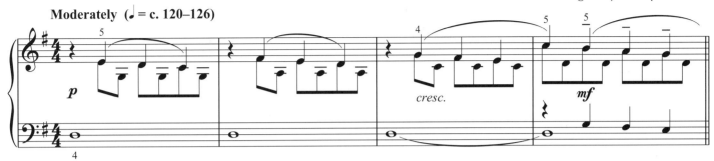

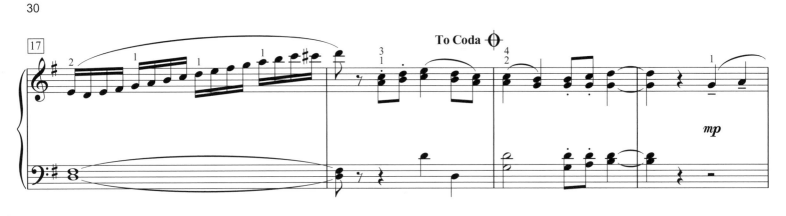

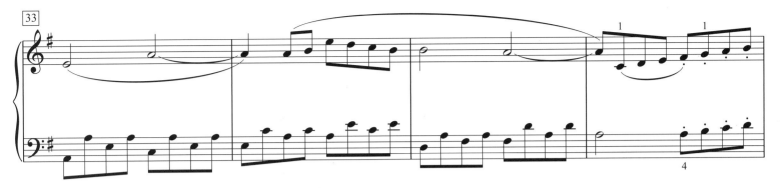

MAKE THE WORLD GO AWAY

Words and Music by
HANK COCHRAN
Arranged by Phillip Keveren

Tenderly (♩ = c. 88)

With pedal

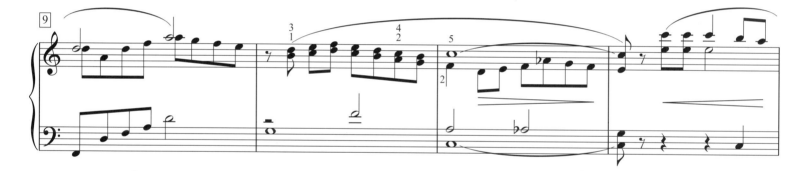

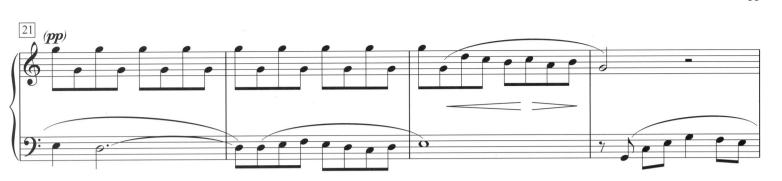

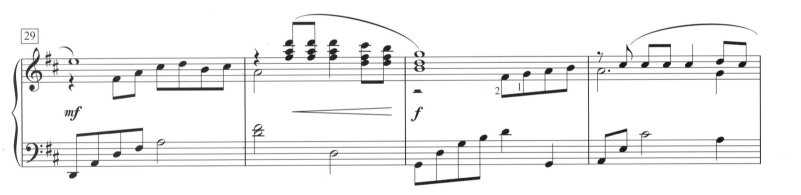

TAKE ME HOME, COUNTRY ROADS

Words and Music by JOHN DENVER,
BILL DANOFF and TAFFY NIVERT
Arranged by Phillip Keveren

Gently flowing (♩ = 69)

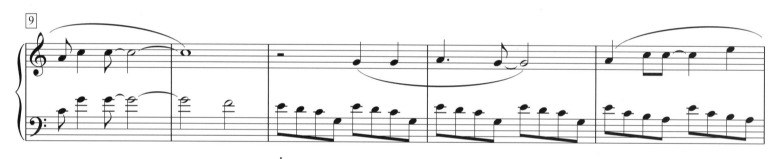

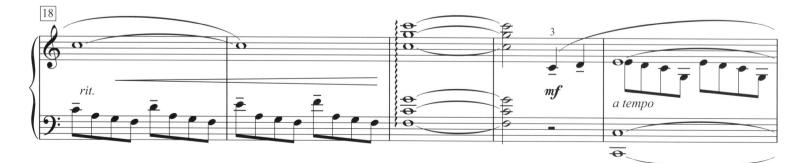

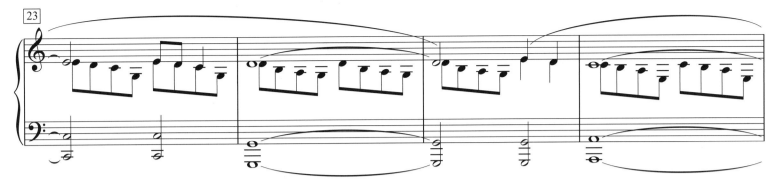

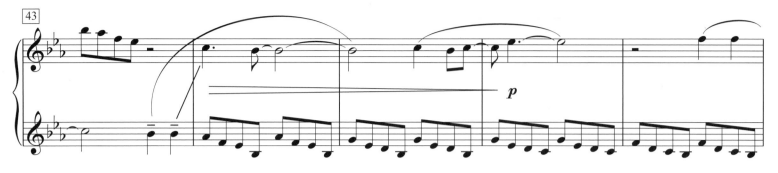

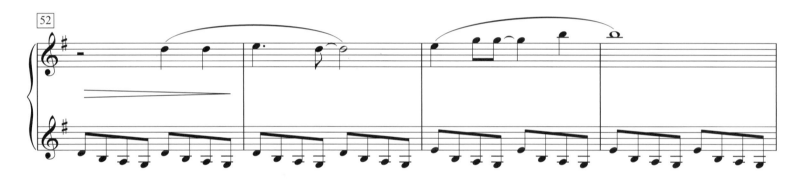

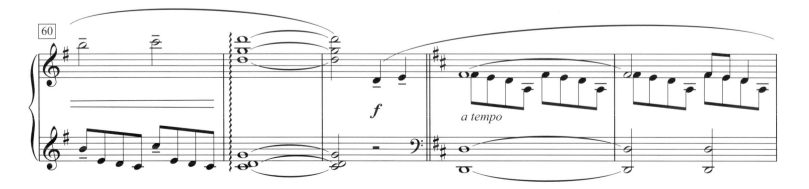

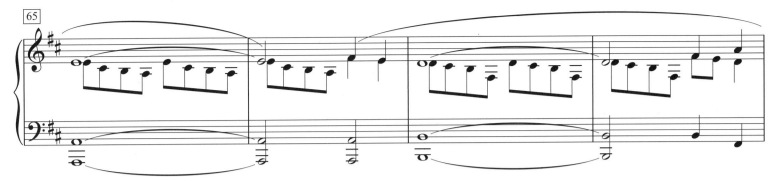

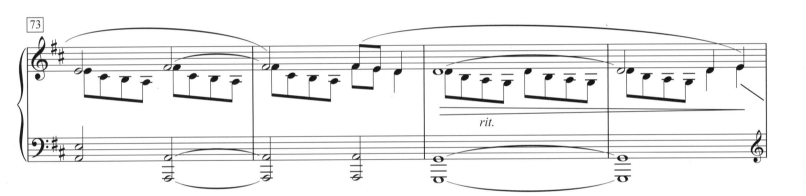

TENNESSEE WALTZ

Words and Music by REDD STEWART
and PEE WEE KING
Arranged by Phillip Keveren

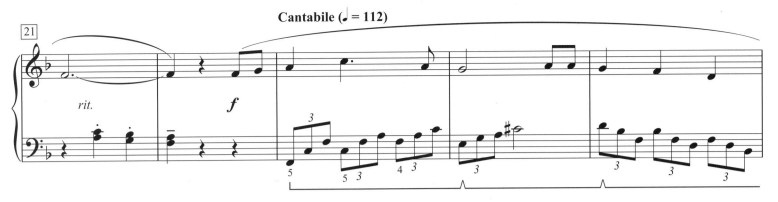

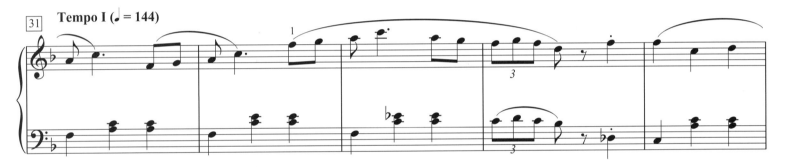

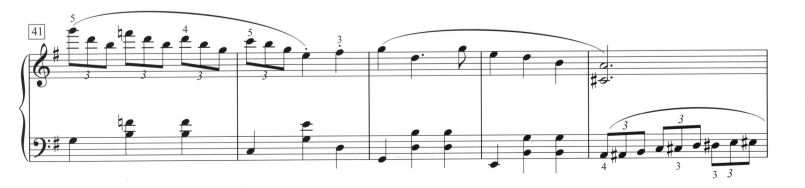

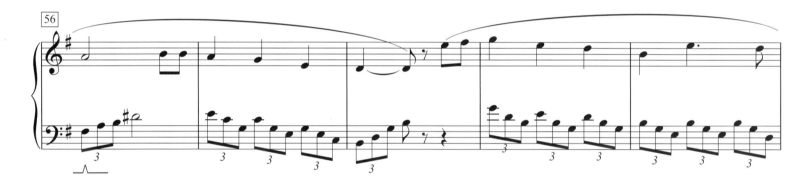

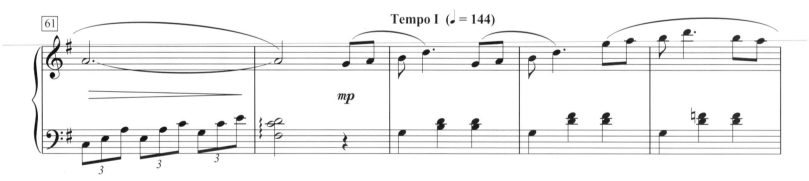

YOU ARE MY SUNSHINE
(Variations)

Words and Music by
JIMMIE DAVIS
Arranged by Phillip Keveren

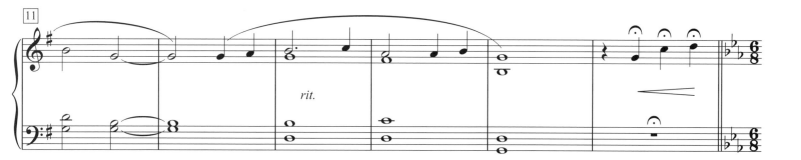

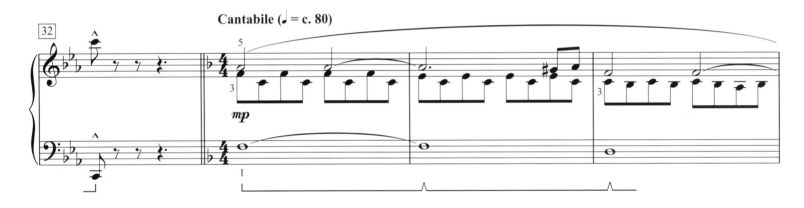

Cantabile (♩ = c. 80)

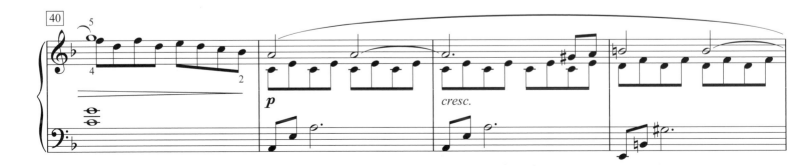

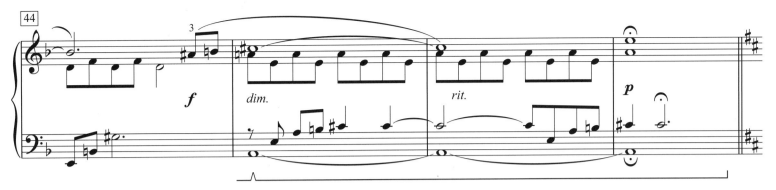

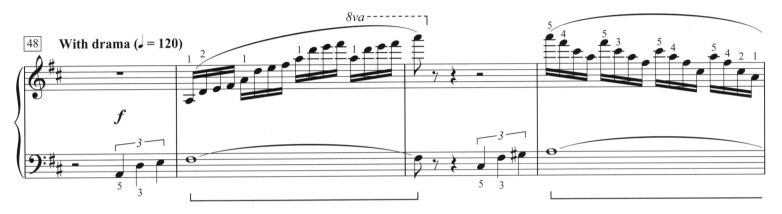

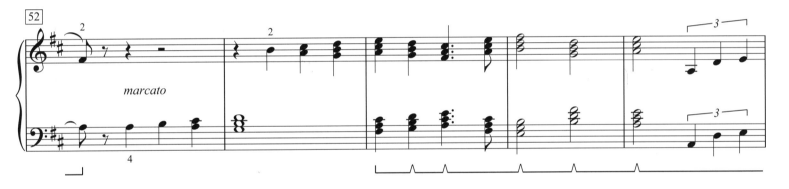

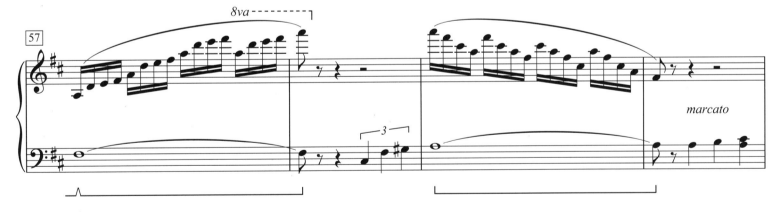

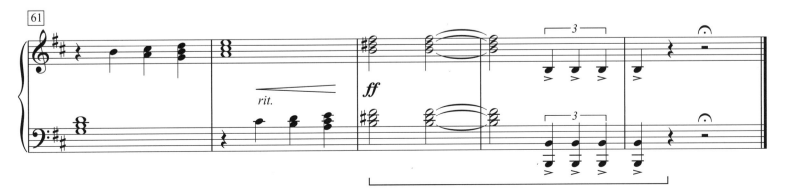

WHY ME?
(Why Me, Lord?)

Words and Music by
KRIS KRISTOFFERSON
Arranged by Phillip Keveren

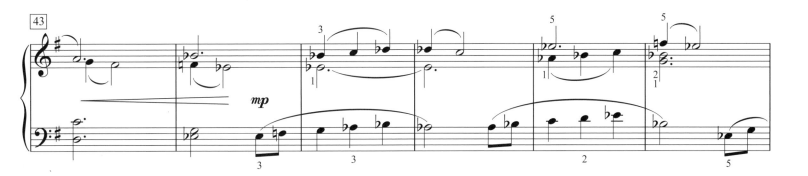

YOUR CHEATIN' HEART

Words and Music by
HANK WILLIAMS
Arranged by Phillip Keveren

Slowly, expressively (♩. = 72)

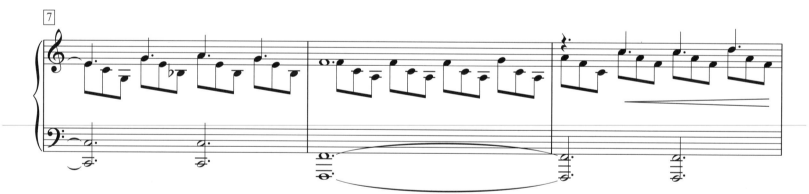

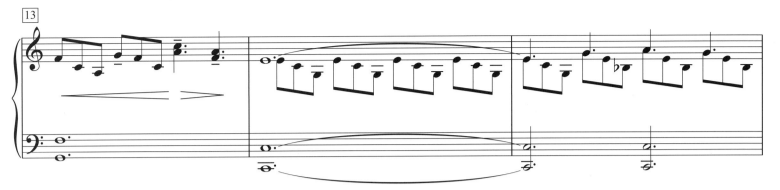

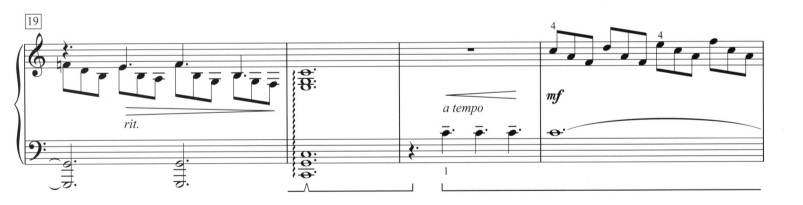

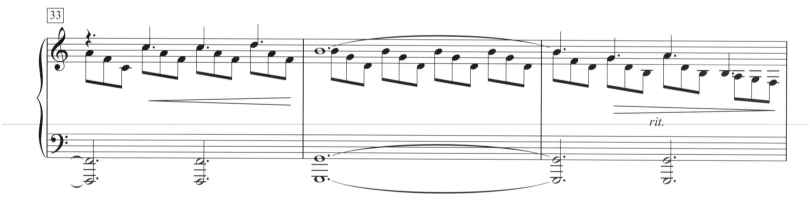

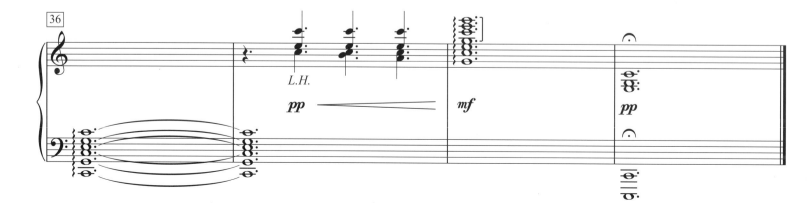